Present
Moment
Meditation

Volume
One

A Journey
of
Self-Discovery

Present Moment Meditation

Volume One

A Journey of Self-Discovery

Kathleen Henning

Publisher's Note

Present Moment Meditation

A Journey of Self-Discovery

By Kathleen Henning

Present Moment Meditation LLC

P. O. Box 530411, Livonia, MI 48153

www.LivinginthePresentMoment.com

This book is dedicated to my loving husband, Bob, my dearest companion and friend.

—Kathleen

Acknowledgments

Thank you to my husband, Bob. Since the early days of Present Moment Meditation, you have been by my side, steady as a rock. Without your support this book would not have been possible. You truly are amazing.

Thank you to my family and friends. Your ongoing support and encouragement mean the world to me.

Thank you to my students for your dedicated participation in our classes, for your commitment to your self-discovery journey, and for your amazing shares and insights. Being with you on this path is an honor. You are an inspiration to us all.

Thank you to the schools and organizations who graciously hosted Present Moment Meditation classes and provided venues that were perfectly suited for us to come together and meditate.

Thank you to the greeters who volunteered their time. Your welcoming smiles and being there for the participants made a big difference to us all.

Thank you to the many teachers who have been my shining star, the guiding light that has shown me the way. You have changed my life beyond what I ever imagined possible, and I am forever grateful.

And finally, *thank you* to my parents, Paul and Dolores, for your love and the sacrifices you made so that I could have a good education and be raised in a community where spirituality and doing the right thing were the standards that we lived by. You provided everything I needed for living a meaningful life. I love you.

Table of Contents

1

HELLO
AND
WELCOME

The miracle of self-discovery is that it transforms our life in the most beautiful ways, from the inside out. It is not a cosmetic fix that fades over time. This transformation is enduring, and its radiance only grows brighter.

"Every block of stone has a statue inside it and it is the task of the sculptor to discover it. I saw the angel in the marble and carved until I set him free."

—Michelangelo

I would like to begin by welcoming you and saying how much I look forward to being with you on the journey that awaits us in the coming pages of this book. It is going to be very exciting.

Exploring who we are as human beings in ways we may not think about very often, or have never thought about before, is one of the most, if not *the* most, meaningful gifts we can give to ourselves. With even the slightest shift in our perspective, or how we approach our life, a whole new world can open up in ways we might never have imagined were possible.

It has been a privilege meeting so many wonderful people who have participated in Present Moment Meditation workshops and classes over the years. I mention them because they are part of the heart and soul of this work.

They are a diverse group, a beautiful cross-section of everyday people just like you and I, encompassing all ages and walks of life—teachers, students, factory workers, engineers, gardeners, business professionals and parents who are working hard and raising families.

At my first meditation class at a local Senior Center there were two participants, Mary and her friend, Anne. Both of them were carrying a cup of coffee as they entered the spacious classroom, which was also the Activities Room used for yoga and the annual Holiday Gift Bizarre that was held every December.

We settled in and I proceeded to tell them my name and a little bit about meditation. I had not gotten very far when Anne turned to Mary and said, "Meditation? I thought you said *medication!*" I laughed and said, "Well, it is—it's just a different kind!"

When class was over, I sat in my car in the Honey Baked Ham parking lot in the summer sunshine and called just about everyone I could think of. I told them about the medication mix-up, and we laughed so hard we could barely catch our breath or utter a word.

To hear the extraordinary, heartfelt shares of my students week after week and be part of their self-discovery journey, plays a meaningful role in my life and for this I am grateful. That might be something you discover for yourself; having meditation companions is inspiring and a great support.

A community of like-minded people is one of the four gatekeepers to the realm of freedom according to, *The Yoga Vasistha*, a meditation text written sometime between the eleventh and fourteenth centuries. The other three which will be mentioned later are: self-inquiry, self-control, and contentment. If we were to look at only these four elements in this book, that in itself would be life changing.

One thing that becomes clear in my classes is how easily we can relate to one another. We realize that we are in this life together with the rest of humanity and all of our 'stuff'. And although we might appear different on the outside, with regards to human nature, we are simply variations on a theme. Same notes, different melodies. Our common human denominator is that we all want the same things—peace and happiness. This book is about that attainment.

At the first session, I invite my students to share why they registered and what benefits they would like to get from the class. As the instructor, I present the course content and guide them into meditation, however, the intentions, self-effort and transformations come from the students themselves.

I am continually surprised and delighted to see how Present Moment Meditation participants are so comfortable when sharing honestly and openly about themselves. They are as real as real can get and this is where the extraordinary meter really ramps up.

There are a variety of reasons for taking a meditation class. They can be funny, heartbreaking, and inspiring. Some of the ones that remain at the top of the popularity charts are: I want to learn how to relax and unwind; to quiet my mind and live in the present moment. I want to stop worrying about the future; lower my blood pressure; and get a good night's sleep.

There are other reasons, as well. Some people are coping with loss and serious health challenges; some just lost their job, while others recently retired and are redesigning their life. Others thought they were empty nesters, but the kids and grandkids are moving back in!

With the fast-paced demands of today's world, people of all ages, from youngsters to senior citizens, are overwhelmed and looking for ways to create stability and balance in their life. Since meditation has become so mainstream, people are curious and want to try it. No longer is meditation reserved for the few who renounce the world and live in a cave high upon a mountaintop, sitting cross-legged in solitude.

Many people who come to my classes want to "discover who I am" and reconnect with themselves inwardly on a deeper level. Others are former meditators from the 1970's who want to reboot their practice with the dynamic energy of group meditation.

As we begin, think about what you would like to discover, what insights or breakthroughs you would like to achieve, or what you want to create for yourself. Whatever you envision, fulfilling any and all of your intentions is possible on your path of self-discovery.

The *Present Moment Meditation Everyday Tools and Practices* that are presented in this book, are specifically designed to be user-friendly and practical so that you can easily incorporate them into your daily activities. Whether you are at home, work, or out-and-about, using the tools will help you stay calm, centered, and present in the moment. They quiet the mind, and when the mind is quiet you are more peaceful and grounded within yourself.

Weaving the tools into your daily routines keeps you aware of and connected to your path. And the more you practice, the easier it is to glide into meditation, as you have maintained the groundwork for turning inward.

Even though the tools are simple, you will soon discover their many benefits and the magical ways they impact your life for the better—and quite often, the lives of those around you. These tools are great supports and companions to have by your side.

Present Moment Meditation is the primary practice that you want to include on your journey. It is the big-daddy of them all. It is the hub, the main power station that sources all of the transformations and beautiful things that will happen along your journey.

Whether you sit for ten minutes or thirty minutes, you will discover that time spent in meditation, turning inward to the quiet place within yourself, adds a wonderful quality to your day. Once you have established a practice, you will notice when you do not meditate; you can tell the difference. I hear that over and over from my students. It is obvious to them when they do not meditate.

The word 'practice' is used a few different ways in this book. It is used as a noun, such as, *meditation practice*, *your practice* and also, *practices*, meaning the tools that you practice. It is also used as a verb meaning, to *practice*. (Whew! It took me a while to practice writing that!)

We will also be using mantras. A mantra is a short phrase that is repeated in conjunction with the breath to help quiet the mind and stay present in the moment. They are also used in meditation.

Every chapter includes a Present Moment Meditation and Everyday Tools and Practices that are specifically designed for that chapter.

Make it a habit to meditate and incorporate the tools into your daily routines. That is how they take root and are there to use and enjoy whenever you need them.

So again, welcome! Let's get started!

Present Moment Meditation
Everyday Tools and Practices
Chapter One – Hello and Welcome

MEDITATION – BREATH AWARENESS

1. In a quiet place, sit comfortably in a chair.

2. Close your eyes. Keep your eyes and all of the muscles around your eyes soft and quiet. This is an important aspect of meditation. Keeping your eyes and the surrounding muscles quiet, reverses the natural tendency of the eyes to look outward. When they are relaxed, you will notice a subtle shift that occurs; the gaze now reflects inward, to the peaceful, quiet space, inside.

3. Place your feet flat on the floor in front of you and directly under your knees.

4. Place your hands on your lap or thighs with the palms upward. Become aware of the openness in the palms of your hands. Relax your fingers.

5. Keep your back straight, but not strained. Relax your entire body, starting with the tip of your toes, rising up through your legs, and your hips. Relax your stomach, rcleasing any tension or tightness; let your stomach be soft. Relax your lower back, waist, and torso. Relax your chest, and continue breathing easy. Relax your shoulders, neck, face, and the top of your head.

6. With your mouth closed, bring your attention to your breath, and gently breathe in and out through your nose at a natural pace. Do not force or change the natural rhythm of your breathing. Breathe in . . . breathe out . . . Ride the wave of your breath, the inhalation and the exhalation, as though it is moving in a circle. Continue with gentle, easy breathing. Lose yourself in your breath. Let your mind melt into your breath.

7. If at any point you become distracted, once again, relax your eyes. Keep them very soft and quiet and return your attention to your breath; ride the wave of your breath, coming in, and going out.

8. Maintain breath awareness.

9. Continue for at least ten minutes.

10. Gently bring your awareness back to your body, back to the room, and slowly open your eyes. Take your time before resuming activity.

PRACTICE

Throughout the day as you go about your activities, pause and become aware of your breath. Keep your attention there for two to three rounds of breathing. This is an easy way to train the mind to stay present in the moment.

Practice this while waiting in line, waiting for the computer to boot up, before a meal, and before bedtime. Be creative, look for opportunities to practice breath awareness and stay present in the moment. Notice the difference it makes!

Meditation Set-up and Guidelines

1. When creating your meditation place, arrange it so that it makes you happy and you look forward to going there. It should be welcoming and conducive to having the best meditation and time with yourself as possible.

2. It is preferable that your place for meditation is in a quiet area, away from activity, televisions, and computers. It can be any size, an entire room or a particular spot in a room. What is important is that you are comfortable there, and it inspires you to meditate.

3. Keep your meditation space clean and uncluttered. Natural or soft lighting works well, as a soft ambiance will help you relax.

4. You can sit in a comfortable chair, or you can sit on the floor. If you decide to use a chair, it is best to choose one without arms so that your body is not constricted. It is best if the back of the chair keeps your posture upright, but not stiff. Also, try to use a chair without any curves in the back that force your posture to bend forward at the waist or any other awkward positions. You do not want to strain or tighten any muscles. To help support your back, you can put a small pillow or a folded towel in the curve of your lower back, near your waistline. This will help keep your torso upright and comfortably support your posture.

5. If you sit on the floor, you can sit on a cushion or a pillow. If you sit cross-legged, you can put a pillow or a

cushion under your knees for support. There are many bolsters and cushions available online and in stores.

6.   Some people prefer to meditate in silence, while others prefer meditative music or recorded guided meditations. It is up to you, just be sure that you are not distracted by whatever you choose, so that the mind can become quiet.

7.   You can wear whatever type of clothing you prefer, however, try to have it be as comfortable as possible, so that you are not distracted.

8.   The best time to meditate is whatever works best for your schedule. The most important thing is to choose a time when you can do it on a regular basis and make it a habit. Many people find that meditating first thing in the morning, before they start their day works well. That way their meditation is the foundation that the rest of their day is built upon. You can also meditate on your lunch hour. A great time to sit quietly, even if only for a short time, is when you get home from work. It will release the busyness of the day and help you unwind, relax, and enjoy your evening meal.

9.   In the evening, before you go to bed, is a beneficial time to meditate. It will relax your body and quiet your mind, supporting you in getting good, restorative sleep. If you awaken in the middle of the night or if your sleep is restless, lie in bed and do some gentle easy breathing.

10.   The length of time you meditate is up to you and whatever works best for your schedule. If you can do twenty minutes, that is great. If ten minutes is all you can

accommodate, that is fine too. Maybe on the weekends or on your days off, you can add fifteen extra minutes.

However many minutes you plan to meditate, sit for that length of time; do not finish sooner just because your body or mind start getting restless. Adding discipline to your practice in this way strengthens your meditation, and also gives you strength when it is required in other areas of life. It increases your ability to stay present in the moment, rather than succumbing to a roaming mind. It supports you when managing challenges, because you stayed the course during your meditation.

And, you will have more patience; a solid foundation in your practice helps carry you through when you thought you had no more to give. If you really want to maximize the opportunity, sit for five minutes longer than you had planned! It will get easier and easier to sit for longer periods of time, and that will make a difference.

11. Do not do any meditation techniques while you are driving, operating machinery, or doing anything that requires your full attention. If you meditate outside of your home, always be sure you are in a safe environment.

12. The more you meditate in your designated place, the more your meditative energy will accumulate there and support you in turning inward. The best approach for meditation is that it is a gift you are giving to yourself.

Y ou don't have to do much to ignite the embers that spark the flame of transformation. A casual willingness or a simple curiosity is enough to start your journey. You can dip your toe in the water and see what happens, or you can run full speed ahead down the wooden planks of the dock and jump in with childlike abandon.

2

MOMENTS
OF
KNOWING

One single moment, one infinitesimal blink of time that passes by, overlooked, can be a turning point that sets us on a path that until then we might never have known existed.

"A journey of a thousand miles must begin with a single step. Do the difficult things while they are easy and do the great things while they are small."

—Lao Tzu

There is a format for writing screenplays that has been used since the early days of filmmaking. It is a sequential outline of necessary elements that are integral for telling the story. It starts with an opening scene and proceeds from there.

In order to create drama in a film, a screenwriter uses what are known as *plot points*, key incidents that take place at specific times that pivot the story into a particular direction and send the main character on their journey. There is drama and relief as the protagonist moves forward throughout the events of the film. And in the process, he or she discovers something about themselves and has a breakthrough, a transformation that culminates in the ending of the story.

If we were to take a look at our life, we would see that there have been numerous plot points that altered the course of our life and sent us in a particular direction—

falling in love, having children, a divorce, getting a PhD, taking a trip around the world, winning the lottery. All the many events that happened along the way brought us to this moment in our life and played a key role in creating the person that we are today.

In 1976, I was in my early twenties and living in Los Angeles, California. I am originally from the Midwest but had flown to San Francisco a couple of years earlier to visit family. As the four-hour plane ride neared its destination and prepared for the final approach, I sprang up and leaned off the edge of my aisle seat so abruptly, you would think someone had just called my name on a game show. What I saw out the windows took my breath away; I had never seen anything like it.

Above, below, and all around, a panorama of pristine, vibrant colors—the brilliant blue sky, the shimmering sapphire water of the San Francisco Bay, and to the north, lush green mountains. And, exquisitely placed like a topper on a wedding cake, was the Golden Gate Bridge, its salmon-colored cables majestically draped, spanning across the mile-wide water, linking the scene together like a human chain of children holding each other's hands. Before the plane landed, I knew I would not be returning home any time soon.

I spent four months in the Bay area exploring the sights, thanks to the gracious hospitality of my aunts and uncles. I worked temporary jobs at Kelly Girl. One of my gigs was at the Lipton Tea Factory, scooping dry onion soup from enormous stainless steel vats into small containers. As I neared the building driving my uncle's yellow pick-up truck, I could smell the sweet aroma of Juicy Fruit gum wafting from the facility next door. Upon leaving, all I could smell were the particles of dehydrated onions stuck in my nose and my hair!

My dear friend, Janet, came out to visit me and with twenty-three dollars in my backpack, we rode the eight-hour bus trip from Santa Cruz to Los Angeles. The bus dropped us off at the corner of Wilshire Boulevard and Rodeo Drive, in the heart of Beverly Hills. I stood on the sidewalk and looked up and down the streets. It felt so familiar, as if I had lived there my entire life.

Janet eventually went back home, and I was now on my own. I got a job working as a waitress in a coffee shop in Santa Monica, just a few blocks from the Pacific Ocean and about a half-hour drive from my adorable studio apartment in West Hollywood. My car, which I named Opal, was a 1948 Dodge with suicide doors and cashmere seats that I had purchased from a little old lady in Pasadena for two-hundred dollars.

One day, I was serving French fries to a man seated at the counter when he looked up at me and said, "You are so good with people, how would you like to be an usherette at CBS television?" Two weeks later I was wearing their uniform, a navy blue blazer, a white blouse and red skirt, escorting audience members to their seats for shows such as *The Price is Right, the Carol Burnett Show, All in the Family,* and *The Sonny and Cher Show.*

It was during this time that I met a guy, Jimmy, in a music class at Los Angeles Community College. I liked him a lot and the more time we spent together the more he felt like my soul mate. He was beautiful, with warm glowing skin. But truth be told, it was not the healthiest relationship. My friend, Belinda, called him a *jive turkey*. I knew she was right, but I did not want to believe her.

One day in June, Jimmy and I were arguing. When I hung up the phone, I knew that it was over. Our relationship was finished, and I was devastated.

I stood alone, empty and frozen. My heart sank to the floor. Actually, it felt as if it fell *through* the floor, and then the floor itself disappeared and I was suspended somewhere in a vacant dark universe.

Who I was in that moment *was* emptiness, as if the only existence that remained of me was a shell with two eyes. But those eyes did not look outward; they stared inward toward the infinite blackness that had become my being. And from the center of that lifeless void arose a powerful, commanding presence that echoed, "Who Am I?"

I could barely move. I was not afraid, but in the absence of my familiar self that I had known just a few moments prior, I did not know what to do.

I walked a few steps forward and fell to my knees. I placed my hands in prayer position on my single bed and prayed the most sincere prayer I have ever uttered, "Please God, tell me why I am here." I stayed there for a while, surrendering myself to a higher power that I had prayed to all my life and now hoped would help me make sense of all of this. I had faith that the divine being could hear me, but I had no expectations. I merely wanted to be comforted by my heavenly friend that I had prayed to, known and trusted, since I was a child.

I stood up and looked out the trio of large windows that faced the u-shaped courtyard that was in the center of the golden age of Hollywood 1930's complex. The sun was shining as I looked up toward the clear blue Southern California sky. In my continued gaze, it was as if I was watching a movie. I could see down the road of my life, a country road bathed in golden hues that extended into the infinite distance that lay before me.

There were no people or things, just the quiet road and the golden light. And then, a rather eerie sensation arose from within and surged through me. It questioned, "Where will I find lasting happiness in this world?"

Belinda was a great friend. She consoled me for as long as I needed, helping me through my tears as I tried to sort out the loss of my relationship with Jimmy.

Later that summer, she spent a week with a meditation teacher who was in the United States from India. Upon her return, on a beautiful sunny day we walked to the nearby park and sat on the grass and she told me about the teacher's message, *"Turn inward ... meditate ... get to know your inner self."*

This was all new to me; I did not know anything about meditation. But in the moment of hearing her words, I immediately recognized without a doubt that what she was telling me was the answer to the prayer that I had whispered while on bended knees just a few months earlier. My heavenly friend had heard me.

As I listened to her speak about meditation, it was as if all the little pockets of 'not-quite-right' that had accumulated inside of me since childhood—braces on my teeth, orthotic saddle shoes instead of trendy penny loafers, curled hair flipping up over my ears instead of cool bangs and long hair draping down to my waist, judging myself against my peers, searching for the perfect boyfriend—were leaving my body one by one and floating away like the translucent soap bubbles that children blow through plastic rings. As the empty pockets were drifting away, they were simultaneously being replaced with a feeling of fullness until no emptiness remained.

Never in my wildest dreams did I imagine that such a boon, gifted from divine compassion, would be granted in such a life-changing way. I was given the answer that I had prayed for, and at that moment, my journey of self-discovery began. I wanted to learn everything that I could about meditation and knowing my self.

One year later, I sold my few possessions and backpacked through Europe on my way to India. In Paris, I heard about the *Magic Bus*, a company of independent bus owners who transported passengers throughout Europe and beyond. For one-hundred-fifty dollars, I booked passage on a bus, similar to a school bus, with an eclectic group of international travelers, and for seven weeks we ventured overland from Paris to New Delhi.

Sometimes we would sleep on the bus which was very uncomfortable, and other times we would find basic accommodations wherever we could. We ran out of gas one beautiful Sunday morning in the Austrian countryside, where an old woman wearing vintage leather ankle boots with tiny buttons, served us breakfast.

We crossed the Black Sea into Turkey, where I had a Turkish bath in Istanbul, and heard the call to prayer from the loudspeakers of mosques throughout the city. On our way out of Turkey, we saw the towering Mount Ararat in the distance, the sixteen-thousand-foot snowcapped mountain mentioned in the Bible and associated with Noah's ark.

We traveled through Iran and into Afghanistan where I drank hot tea with the locals. Nearing closer to our final destination we entered Pakistan, where people that I had just met invited me to their outdoor wedding reception.

A few days later, we arrived in New Delhi, with its colorful, crowded streets, where ancient temples and traditions mixed with the modern world.

From there, it was off to the ashrams and meditation centers, where I would live full-time, immersing myself in the study and practice of meditation. Over the next ten years, I would return to India two more times.

Present Moment Meditation
Everyday Tools and Practices
Chapter Two – Moments of Knowing

MEDITATION – EMBRACING THE PAST

1. Follow steps 1-8 on page 21-22 (in Chapter One)

2. Imagine that your chest cavity, or your entire body, is filled with empty space, like the inside of a large vase, or an inflated balloon. Now, gently become aware of your past. Do not intentionally recollect any specific images or events, just maintain an overall ambiance and awareness that you have a past. Breathe easy and stay relaxed. If any images or scenes from your past appear, acknowledge them, and let them float by like clouds in a summer sky. Whatever shows up, let it be. Let it come, and let it go. Do not judge anything. If any emotions arise, notice them and let them pass by. Remain detached and simply observe, as if you are watching a movie.

3. Continue for at least ten minutes.

4. Before you open your eyes, send a blessing of peace to your past. Thank your past, smile at your past, wave good-bye to your past, say a prayer for your past. Embrace your past with open arms, or in whatever way you would like to graciously acknowledge all the parts of your past.

5. Take your time, and finish up.

6. Gently bring your awareness back to your body and back to the room, and slowly open your eyes. Take a few moments before resuming activity.

PRACTICE

1. Make peace with your past, whatever that means for you, whether it was ten years ago or ten minutes ago. Let what is past remain in the past and keep moving forward, just as the river continually ventures onward. It is not held back in any way by its past or where it has been. It only flows forward, unrestricted, bending with the twists and turns of the banks.

2. If there is anything from your past that is unfinished business that you would like to complete so that you can move on and be free from it, this is a great opportunity to do so. It might be a phone call to acknowledge to your friend that you said you would take them to lunch and you did not follow through with your invitation. Or, it might mean that in your heart you forgive yourself or someone else for something that was said or done. Whether you choose to interact with another person or complete it within yourself, keep in mind that in the process, there is no blame or judging allowed; neither for yourself, someone else, or with regards to what happened. That only keeps it hanging around, which is not the result that you want. Acknowledge yourself for taking action. It will free up space both within you, and on your journey of self-discovery.

W e want to be happy. We want to be at peace. We want to be fulfilled. When we seek this experience from the outside world, it is temporary, it comes and goes, sometimes lasting longer than other times, but always moving, like the wind. That is the nature of the physical world.

3

HEADING
IN A
NEW DIRECTION

The one extraordinary journey that cannot be found in travel guides is the journey of self-discovery. This is a journey that takes a person deep within themselves, to a destination of serene peace and contentment.

"When you are inspired by some great purpose, some extraordinary project, all your thoughts break their bonds. Dormant forces become alive, and you discover yourself to be a greater person by far than you ever dreamed yourself to be."

—Patanjali

S ince the days of Jimmy and feeling as if my heart had fallen through the floor, I can tell you that who I used to be is not who I am today. Not even close. If I do say so myself, the transformation has been absolutely incredible. The young woman who lived in Hollywood on Formosa Avenue has come a long way. Her journey was not always easy, but it was quite remarkable.

Undoubtedly, maturing had a lot to do with it, but the added dimension in my personal growth was due to the journey that awakened me to my self, the journey of turning inward. Because of meditation and practicing self-reflection, I know who I am—regardless of what my mind chatter sometimes wants me to believe. I know that it is up to me to choose what thoughts I will listen to and allow to linger and loop over and over in my mind like repetitive elevator music, and which ones I will not.

I am grounded in the awareness that regardless of the circumstances, there is a 'me' inside that is always steady and unaffected by change. And despite what transpires on any given day, I know that my essence is peace and contentment and everything else is like clothing I wear that hides that essence. I understand that I will have ups and downs because we live in a world of fluctuation and instability, and sometimes the waves are bigger than I would prefer. But at the end of the day, my inner home is there waiting for me.

Even if I am upset or frustrated, I know that beneath the layer of emotions there is a place within the very heart of my being that is not affected by the coming and going of the tides, and that enduring peace is who I am. All the ups and downs in my life are vehicles for me to learn, to sharpen my skills as I navigate my way. I cannot control or change the world; all I can do is manage as best as I can, the ways in which I engage with it.

Who I am today may not be how I experience myself tomorrow, or the next day, or the day after that. As time passes and I stay committed to my meditation journey, I become a happier and more contented version of me. The path of self-discovery is a continual unfolding, and it is a beautiful thing. It is made by placing one foot in front of the other, by stepping down and moving forward. Typical of pathways, they are not always linear; they might meander and sometimes arrive at a fork in the road. But as long as we stay true to our goal, everything will be fine.

You never know when the call to turn inward will come. You cannot predict what events of life will bring you to the doorstep of a journey that will illuminate such great discoveries about yourself. Once you place your foot down and take that first step, something miraculous happens. A shift occurs, and although it might not be obvious, you are headed in a new, exciting direction.

What is so wonderful about this path is that the insights that are revealed and what you will learn along the way do not require anything outside of your normal scope of daily living.

You do not have to go anywhere special to practice. All you have to do is keep meditating and everything else will take care of itself. How much simpler can it be?

Your personal journey starts when you take the first step, and it begins exactly where you are right now. It includes all the conditions and situations in your life—past, present and future. It includes those characteristics that you like about yourself, and those which you would like to improve upon. It is fine whether you are light-hearted, serious, or indifferent, or whether you live in a palace or a hut in the forest. None of this matters, it is all perfect and all part of the journey. You are at a very meaningful starting point and that is what is important.

Embrace everything that has brought you to this point in your life, all of it. Embrace your magnificence, your splendor and your shortcomings, the comfortable and the uncomfortable. It is all welcome. What you will come to discover is that anything that prohibits you from experiencing contentment and peace of mind must eventually go. Anything that is not meant to stay will effortlessly fall away.

As you meditate and practice self-awareness, transformations will take place, changes that unfold within you that will affect your life in positive ways. They will happen naturally in the course of day-to-day living—while you are at work, studying for an exam, grocery shopping, taking care of your children, caring for your elderly parents, building a bigger home, or downsizing to a smaller one.

Sometimes the changes are subtle. Perhaps you smile more because you discover that it helps you stay relaxed. Other changes may be more obvious and dramatic—you decide to go for it, quit your anxiety-ridden job and find a career that is more suited to your liking. It is all up to you. It is your journey.

You will soon find that there is no shortage of opportunities to practice; life is generous that way. There will always be situations that arise that require extra patience, acceptance, and steadiness of mind, all of which are strengthened with a practice of meditation and by using the Present Moment Meditation Tools.

As soon as you start meditating, you will notice a difference; it does not take long to see the results. For instance, driving in traffic might not be as stressful as it used to be. You are able to remain calm which in turn, benefits your health. You might find that by altering your approach to tasks that were once mundane or that you resented doing, are now more enjoyable. Or that by giving up your need to control, you are more at ease and experience more freedom within yourself. You might also find that when you meditate, you sleep better than you have in years.

You might discover that the more you stay present in the moment, the easier it is to accept those things in life that you cannot change, and as a result, there is more flow and happiness in your life. Even slight adjustments can make a world of difference. Like pennies in a bank, they all add up!

One of my students who had been meditating regularly for a few years, was hosting Thanksgiving dinner for her large family. In addition to the usual turkey, stuffing, mashed potatoes, and gravy, she prepared all kinds of special dishes. For whatever reasons, half of her guests arrived almost two hours late. Rather than getting upset, which prior to meditating would have been her modus operandi, she warmly welcomed the late arrivals, and with regards to the food which by now was somewhat dry she laughed and said, "Put more gravy on it!"

Little by little, like anything else, practicing is the key. At some point you will look back and say, "Wow, I have changed. I don't worry as much as I used to," or "I see that I am making healthier lifestyle choices and feel so much better," or "I am so much more patient, and that has made a big difference in my relationship with my family." Sometimes you will not be able to pinpoint when the shift occurred; all you know is that it did. And that is part of the magic; transformation naturally happens just by applying a few simple practices to your daily life.

Nurture your practice and it will nurture you. Your practice will *always* have your best interest at heart and will *always* have your back. It will never let you down. The more you stay in tune with your path, the more you become one with it. In essence, your path *is* you! So, take good care of it.

Present Moment Meditation
Everyday Tools and Practices
Chapter Three – Heading in a New Direction

MEDITATION – EMBRACE ALL THAT YOU ARE

1. Follow steps 1-8 on page 21-22 (in Chapter One)

2. Relax your entire body. Fill your whole being with peace and contentment, allowing them to permeate every pore of your being. Now, within this space of peace and contentment, embrace all that you are, everything; the parts that you love about yourself, and those that you would like to change. For now, they are equally acceptable, embrace them all. Embrace all that you have done, and the many ways that you have given of yourself and served others. Acknowledge your life and all that it is today, exactly as it is. Embrace the present moment.

3. Continue for at least ten minutes.

4. Before you open your eyes, bless yourself. Bless your life, all of it. Acknowledge yourself. Bless all of the people in your life. Bless your community. Thank yourself, and bless yourself for all that you do.

5. Take your time, and finish up.

6. Gently bring your awareness back to your body and back to the room, and slowly open your eyes. Take a few moments before resuming activity.

PRACTICE

1. As you go about your day and move forward on your journey, be aware of the many components that comprise your life—family and friends, health and exercise, food and drink, career and finances, your home, aspirations and goals, spiritual and personal enrichment. Notice how each of them impact your well-being, happiness and peace of mind. Are there any that you have outgrown and no longer have a place or useful purpose in your life? Is it time for other areas of your life to rise to the top of your list? Perhaps the time has come for you to give them your attention.

2. Pick one or two areas in your life that you would like to change for the better, even if it is only a slight adjustment, and take action. Continue following through, bringing it to fruition, and be sure to acknowledge yourself along the way.

There is no end to what can be discovered within the realm of your being. Your journey is a beautiful process, like the unfolding of a spring flower, timely and right on track. One step at a time, one day at a time, one breath at a time.

<u>4</u>

THE GIFT
OF
MEDITATION

Let your meditation practice take its natural course. Something beneficial is always transpiring, so do not give up. Be patient and keep practicing. Who knows what awaits you in your next meditation!

*"Learn to carry all the conditions of happiness
and peace within yourself by meditating and attuning your
consciousness to the ever-existing, ever-new joy
of your inner self. Meditate more and more deeply,
until joy becomes second nature to you."*

—Yogananda

When Belinda told me about the teacher's message, *"Turn inward ... meditate ... get to know your inner self,"* what was it about that instruction that had me instinctively know that it was the answer to my prayer? Why did it resonate so deeply within me? Why did those words ring so true at the very core of my being? What was it about that message that I knew I had to pursue and learn more about?

Over thousands of years, a great number of books have been written by masters of meditation, in many different languages, countries and cultures throughout the world. Regardless of the words they used or the methods they taught, many of them share a common bond and allude to one central idea—that meditation is a vehicle for anyone wanting to find lasting happiness and peace.

Since the beginning of time, humankind has endured struggle and hardship, both individually and collectively. This is part of living in a world that is constantly changing and encompasses differences and duality, the pairs of opposites. Duality is everywhere, some examples are you and me, right and wrong, day and night, rich and poor, love and hate, birth and death. Within these polarities are the extremes and everything in-between.

Searching for lasting happiness and stability while living amidst the opposites has always been a key pursuit for human beings. It is as though we intrinsically want to claim, or reclaim, a part of ourselves that seems to be missing, so that we can live with a fulfilled sense of self.

That claiming is what happens in meditation. Lasting peace cannot be found if we look for the source of it outside of ourselves in a world of change and instability. That is the glitch in the caboodle. We have been looking in the wrong direction. And that is why we are instructed by the meditation masters to look within.

One of my favorite teachings from an early meditation text is, "Wake up, wake up! Come to know your own self!"

According to the masters, the self, the subtle realm of consciousness within, is the essence of who we are. It is present within the body, but at the same time, is separate from it. It is the part of us that gives life to the body, mind, and senses. Without this self the heart would not beat, the mind would not think, and the skin would be devoid of sensations.

The self is the source of creativity and love, joy and compassion, contentment and kindness. It is beyond the thinking mind and is never disturbed by mental agitation or fluctuating emotions. It dwells at the innermost part of our being and when we are in touch with it is when we feel the most fulfilled.

It is a wonderous way to live life, knowing that even when we are babysitting or raking leaves, the experience of being fulfilled and content is always present within us.

Most importantly, the nature of the inner self is that it is *unchanging*. That alone is worth its weight in gold. Imagine that inside our body, which also undergoes constant change, there is an aspect of ourselves that never changes, and remains infinitely at peace and content within itself. There is nowhere else in the world that anything unchanging can be found.

And that is why we meditate. That is why we stay present in the moment and weave our practices into our daily life, so that we can stay awake and maintain our inner connection. And as I mentioned before, even when we forget and get lost in the swirl of life, it does not matter. Our inner self is still there, always there, in its pure, unchanging state of being.

When we sit for meditation and turn inward, we tap into that source and are reminded of our most dear, precious relationship with our inner self. And while we are there visiting, we are restored and rejuvenated.

One of the most incredible gifts that we receive in meditation is that we have the experience that we are whole and complete within ourselves, because our inner self is always whole and complete, and that is an incredible, life-changing experience. It is transforming and sets us in a new direction. There is a shift in who we know ourselves to be, and we are never the same. This experience, this awakened knowledge, grows deeper and deeper as a result of our commitment to our practice.

Any time we feel empty or out-of-sorts, the mere knowing that our inner self is whole and complete, even if we are not feeling that way at the time, will carry us through and put us back on track. Step by step, we learn and grow, and that is why the journey of self-discovery is always fresh, wonderful, and enriches our lives.

Meditation is when you spend time with yourself at the deepest level of your being, the very heart and soul of who you are. When the body is relaxed, the mind is quiet and your attention is turned inward, there is a feeling of love. At times, it feels as if love fills every pore of your body.

When you rest in this awareness it feels intimately close to you; you feel closer to your self than you ever have before. Many of my students describe this experience by saying, "It feels like I have come home."

This is because there is a recognition that your inner self is a part of you that you have known before, but somehow fell out of touch with, and have been searching for ever since. It is as though you are seeing yourself reflected in a mirror. Not the kind of reflection you see when you are fixing your hair or tweaking your outfit. This reflection is soul to soul, heart to heart, no pretenses; it is the real deal.

You realize that this experience of love is not just a feeling. It is the very essence of who you are. It is not separate or different from you, it *is* you. How do we know this to be true? By meditating. Even if just for a moment you capture a glimpse, that is enough. And the more you meditate and strengthen your relationship with your inner self, the more this relationship will become a foundation in your life and something that you cherish.

The energy of meditation often manifests as deep inner silence and peace and can also express itself in other ways according to each individual person. Whatever happens in your meditation is perfect for you and what is meant to be. And the same is true for me and everyone else.

Let go of any expectations about what you think should or should not happen when you meditate. Do not try to force anything; to do so would require the involvement of your mind and that would be counterproductive. You are not guiding your meditation, your inner self is. So step aside, get out of your own way, and let it do its work.

In many cultures, shoes are not allowed to be worn inside meditation halls. Foot attire is left outside or in overcrowded shoe rooms. It is a good idea to remember where you put your shoes, otherwise, it is like standing in the middle of a busy parking lot trying to remember where you parked your car.

At one of the centers where I stayed, there was a sign outside the meditation hall that read, "Leave your ego with your shoes." An adaptation of this that I share with my students prior to meditation is, "Let go of your need to control before you sit for meditation."

Take advantage of this golden opportunity to do nothing, except be with yourself and enjoy the quiet stillness. All you have to do is sit comfortably, close your eyes, breathe easy, and turn within. How extraordinary that something so life-changing can be so simple!

Your meditations may not always be the same. One time you might find yourself going over your shopping list in your head. Another time you might be thinking about the pile of work sitting on your desk at the office. Or you might find yourself in a deep, thought-free state where you are completely at peace. Sometimes, your mind is quiet, and you are present in the moment, present with your self.

Meditation can sometimes feel like sleep; however, it is not sleep. Meditation is a different level of consciousness where the body, mind and senses are completely still. For many years, my meditations felt like I was in a deep, quiet place within myself. I was out like a light—my head falling forward and my body leaning to one side. But I was not asleep. This was all part of the process and the inner workings of transformation.

Even though I had only meditated for approximately forty-five minutes, when I came out of meditation I was so rejuvenated that it felt as if I had slept for eight hours. Just twenty minutes of meditation can be incredibly refreshing and restorative.

Maybe you, like many of my students, do not sleep well due to worry or the inability to quiet the mind. If you actually do fall asleep while meditating, that is perfect and exactly what your body needs. So stay with it and trust yourself, your body, and your meditations.

It is common for meditators, whether beginners or long-time practitioners, to think that they should not have any thoughts during their meditation. This is a lofty endeavor, but not a very practical one.

During meditation, thoughts will come and go. Sometimes they are prominent, boldly marching across the screen in the foreground of your mind. If that happens, do not worry about it. Simply guide your attention back to your breathing and ride the wave of your breath.

At other times thoughts may be distant, almost transparent, with little voice or meaning. They fade into the background of your awareness and remain there, barely noticeable like a backdrop in a stage play.

Meditations sometimes go like this: there is thinking, and then there is no-thinking. There is thought, and then there is no-thought. You are aware that you are meditating, and then you are not aware that you are meditating.

And here is the awesome part; in-between thinking and no-thinking, and in-between being aware and not being aware, there is a gap, an infinitesimal silent space where you are completely free. It is difficult to describe the richness that is experienced in the gap, this deep state of meditation. Later, upon reflection, you will realize that you did indeed have moments when you were completely absorbed in consciousness, in the gap.

When coming out of meditation, there is often a sense of euphoric stillness. As you transition from the tranquil inner world to the activity of the outer world, you may also have the feeling that you went somewhere, that during meditation you were transported to another realm inside yourself. This is true, you were.

You might think from time to time that your meditations are not working because nothing seems to be happening. You may doubt yourself and come to the conclusion that you must be doing something wrong, that you are not doing it correctly. But thinking that your meditations are not working is wrong understanding. Let these kinds of thoughts go. They have no meaning, are of no importance, and will only hinder your progress. Judging is the voice in your head that says, "if only this, then..." or, "if only that, then..." This meaningless mind chatter does nothing to forward your meditation practice or your journey of self-discovery. So, do not go there.

Rest assured, when you sit for meditation something is always happening inside, at a deeper level of your being. However, it can be so subtle that you may not notice it. Every time you meditate, every time you practice staying present in the moment, every time you apply one of the

Present Moment Meditation Tools, you are gently wiping away the dross until only the best version of you remains.

At the end of winter just before the dawn of spring, trees look bleak and appear to have little to no life in them. But as the weather warms and sunshine is seen more frequently, tiny buds appear on the barren branches. And not long after, the buds blossom into flowers and leaves are soon to follow.

All the while, we thought nothing was happening with the tree. But our thinking was in error. Underneath the snow and the frozen ground, a lot was happening. The tree was undergoing a miraculous transformation, we just could not see it. The same is true with your meditations. Even when you think nothing is happening, you are undergoing a miraculous transformation.

You will see the benefits of your self-effort manifesting in your life while you take care of the many things that you do on any given day. I promise you that. Time devoted to your practice always pays off big time. Every minute spent in meditation is an investment in your well-being, your happiness, and your journey of self-discovery.

Turning inward allows you to take a break and distance yourself from your thoughts and daily routines. In doing so, you gain a fresh perspective on life. Not only will you feel different, you might also look different. People who know you or see you on a regular basis might look at you with a slightly furrowed brow while leaning in closer to ask, "Did you do something different with your hair?"

They cannot quite put their finger on it, but they can see that something is different. What is it about you that has changed?

"Oh, no!" you enthusiastically reply. "I started meditating!"

"That's what it is!" they smile and say, nodding their head in agreement. They recognize that what they were noticing as something different is the extra sparkle in your eyes and the quality of calmness that surrounds you.

Present Moment Meditation
Everyday Tools and Practices
Chapter Four – The Gift of Meditation

MEDITATION – YOU ARE HOME

1. Follow steps 1-8 on page 21-22 (in Chapter One)

2. Relax your entire body. As you breathe in and breathe out, become aware of the subtlety of your breath. Let go of any bodily sensations. Now, focusing on the in-breath, let it carry you deep inside, to the center of your being. On the exhale, release and let go. Again, as you breathe in, ride the wave of your in-breath, letting it take you to your center, to your inner self. Go deep. When you arrive there, take a seat, you are home. Be with your self and the peace and tranquility that reside there.

3. Continue for at least ten minutes.

4. Before you open your eyes, make an imprint inside yourself, exactly where the center of your being is, so that you know exactly where to connect with your self, your inner home, any time, day or night.

5. Take your time, and finish up.

6. Gently bring your awareness back to your body and back to the room, and slowly open your eyes. Take a few moments before resuming activity.

PRACTICE

1. During the day, be aware of that place inside yourself that you experienced in meditation; your center, the home of your self. That center is your core, your solid footing that keeps you present in the moment and grounded as you go about your daily activities. It is always near, right there inside. Any time you would like, you can ride your in-breath to the center of your being and reconnect, restore and refresh.

2. Riding the wave of your breath, and using the in-breath to take you to the center of your being, is great to do at bedtime, or before falling asleep. Also, if you wake up during the night or your sleep is restless, do this practice. It is very calming, quiets the mind, and will help you get a good night's sleep.

♪ RAPP ♪

Repeat this to yourself.

Regularity: One of the key building blocks for maintaining my meditation practice is regularity. Consistency keeps my practice alive and healthy and I am less likely to drift astray and fall back into old patterns and habits. With regular practice the restlessness of my mind is tamed, and I am able to stay present in the moment.

Acceptance: I approach my meditations with a graceful demeanor. I enter my practice with open arms and humility, relinquishing my willfulness, knowing that whatever happens is perfect and divinely guided.

Patience: Whatever I am meant to experience in my meditations will unfold exactly when and how they are supposed to, so I will be patient. Nothing I can do will change its natural course. Applying patience to my practice carries over into my life and will be there whenever I need it. I will keep practicing, embrace where I am, and trust my process.

Practice: I want my meditations to be firmly established and continue bearing magnificent fruit. I will maintain my practice so that I can skillfully maneuver the ups and downs of life. All I have to do is keep practicing. How fortunate I am that I can practice amidst my everyday activities!

From an early age, I sensed that there was something more, some aspect of myself that I had not yet come to know. But I had no clue what it was or how to inquire as to what it might be. Only in meditation did I find what was missing, what I knew in every fiber of my being to be true. There <u>was</u> something more.

5

ROLES
AND
IDENTITIES

*There are things that we did, or
said, that if given the chance to do
over, we might do differently. But
at the time, we did the best we
could. How do we know that?
Because that is what we did.*

"In every moment, we are in that field of all possibilities where we have access to an infinity of choices. The most creative act you will ever undertake is the act of creating yourself."

—Deepak Chopra

If the self is our essence and always present within us, and its nature is enduring love, kindness, and all of the other qualities that human beings strive for, how can there be unhappiness? There would be no reason for people to say, "I want to find myself," or "I don't know who I am." Let us take a closer look.

On the day we were born, we arrived pure and innocent. Our precious hands and tiny fingers were barely able to grasp. Our eyes were not yet open. And little by little over time, we grew and developed, formulating an identity and evolving into a multi-faceted individual that encompassed all of the wonders and magnificence that a human being entails.

This includes a physical body, a mind and the capacity to think, five senses, memory, a wide spectrum of emotions, and much more. With these factors we put together our 'self', what we often think of as our identity.

Add to the mix the world around us—the powerful dynamic of family, our heritage and traditions, our schooling, occupations and economic status, our network of friends, societal trends, and so much more. There is a lot of influence going on. As we mature, our identity is further shaped by our accomplishments and failures, beliefs and opinions, and our appearance, professions, and possessions.

Of course, our identity also includes our quirks and idiosyncrasies. I am happy to mention a few of my own! I like things in place, no street shoes worn on the carpet, and most importantly, absolutely no pickles served with my tuna melt. They stink. I do not want to be within a mile of a pickle, and I definitely do not want their stinky juice soaking into my sandwich!

To say that human beings are complicated would be an understatement. All of these various components, from the moment of birth until now, collectively bundled together are the sum total of the person that we have become and what we call, *me*. Although these components influence who we are, it is how we relate to them that is most important. Because how we relate to them creates who we know and believe ourselves to be. This is where we want to be very careful.

Contemplating who we are in relationship to all of these factors can be an eye-opening, liberating experience, and free us up in ways we might not have known were available. Typically, we think that these identities *are* who we are, rather than separate entities unto themselves. We think that who we are is this compilation of parts and pieces, yet none—not one iota, zip, zero, nada—of these have anything to do with our inner self, the unchanging presence within.

They are simply elements in the dance ensemble of life, and your role as one of the dancers is to dance freely with full self-expression with the awareness that who you are, is the conscious presence *within* the dancer, and not the tuxedo, the tutu, or the tap shoes. Nor are you the music; you are, however, the maestro of your own symphony.

Living as our identities without knowing our inner self can be confusing, frustrating and even disheartening at times, as our created identities conflict with our inner truth. This conflict is a source of unhappiness and one of the reasons that people question who they are and search to find themselves.

Through gentle self-inquiry, which is part of our practice and one of the four gatekeepers, we are able to identify how and in what ways we are confined or restricted by influences that at the time they occurred, may or may not have been of our own choosing. Once we shed light on them and see them for what they are— something that happened, something that was said—we can release their grip on us.

This is transformation. This is how we free ourselves and experience peace not only during meditation, but in our daily life. This is what the masters are referring to when they speak about bondage and liberation. This is what they mean when they implore us, again and again, to, "Wake up!" Come to know your own self!" And this is why the message that Belinda shared resonated so deeply within me. My self was calling to be known.

Whatever your roles are in life, with an awareness of self there is more freedom to navigate amidst the innumerable diversities of the universe, what is known in Taoism as, *the ten thousand things.* You can confidently travel forward on your path, knowing who you are and who you are not.

Many factors that influence us and become part of our identity come from outside of ourselves, beginning in our formative years and continuing through adulthood. They shape how we portray ourself, our self-confidence, our ability to love and be loved, and so much more. These influences can be significant or insignificant, long lasting or short lived. An influence that contributes to our identity can be something as simple as a compliment, as awe-inspiring as summiting Mount Everest, or as trivial as being a contestant on a game show.

In 1987, my husband and I were planning a trip to Los Angeles and I thought it would be fun to be a contestant on, "Wheel of Fortune." I liked the show, plus, having worked on game shows while at CBS Television, I knew exactly what the producers were looking for in a contestant—happy, energetic, and easy to interact with. No problem, that sounds easy enough.

In fact, while at CBS, I was given a ticket to be a contestant on, "Let's Make a Deal." I borrowed an Irish peasant dress from the wardrobe department, painted a shamrock on my cheek, and off I went in my '48 Dodge. I smiled and cheered and was chosen to play and before long I was standing beside Monty Hall, the host of the show. He gave me the choice of curtain number one or the box on Jay's tray. I picked the tray and came home four-hundred dollars richer!

So, how hard could "Wheel" be? I applied, took the test, and was chosen to be on the show. I shopped for the perfect outfit and practiced playing the game as much as I could, including during the plane ride out west.

At the television studio, before taping began, a man who was one of the producers met with me and the other contestants in a small room. He gave us some tips to help us relax and ensure that everything would run smoothly. One point that he emphasized numerous times was, "Whatever you do, do *not* buy a vowel that was already bought. The people at home get upset and throw things at their television because they think we pick contestants who aren't very smart to be on the show." Okay, I got this.

It was game time and they called my name. I stood in my spot behind the giant wheel, between a brunette woman to my left, and a guy to my right. Pat and Vanna were very friendly, chatting with the live studio audience and us, the players. Then, BOOM, the lights went bright, and it was show time. We took turns spinning the wheel and guessing letters and the woman to my left was winning everything.

It was then my turn, I decided to go for it, "Pat, I'd like to buy an 'A'." The place suddenly froze as if an artic chill had just blown through the room. I stood motionless in front of the cameras like a deer in the headlights, realizing that although an 'A' was not showing on the game board, it had already been bought. Pat was as kind as could be, while I was sure that the clamor I heard in the audience was my husband crawling under his chair!

Needless to say, I did not win. The woman to my left took home all the prizes and the loot. I would have been happy with the three-foot high ceramic Dalmatian that was a popular prize on the show, but it was not meant to be. My consolation prize was a four-foot high, ornate Italian lamp with a young lad and maiden gracefully peeking around a tree, adoring each other beneath a fountain of teardrop shaped crystals. During the commercial break, Pat went to bat for me and asked the producers, "Kathy seems like a very nice woman, isn't there something else we can give her?" Nope.

I called my father back home and bless his heart, he tried to console me as best as he could. My husband was not quite sure what to say. I did not tell anyone when the show was airing. It took my game show contestant identity quite a while to recover!

Factors that shape us can also come from inside ourselves, when we make up interpretations and stories about what did or did not happen; we put a spin on them, elaborating and fabricating. And then, we believe that what we made up is true. This is where things really get dicey. Once we start concocting a story, the voice in our head, which is part of the mind, chimes in with its opinion, adding spice to the mix, evidence that either validates or invalidates our concoction. This further reinforces our story, making it seem that much more believable, and giving it a false sense of reality. I could create all kinds of dramatic interpretations about my "Wheel of Fortune" experience, but in reality, all that happened was that I bought an 'A' that had already been played. Everything else that is added to that is made up, it is a story.

Whatever your interpretations are, and whatever meaning and importance you give to them, are what determines your experience of yourself, your life, your peace of mind, and every minute of every day. This process of occurring, assimilating and assessing takes place so fast that unless you are present in the moment and vigilant in your practice, most of the time you will not even realize it is happening. This is why it is so important to meditate. This is why you want to be committed to your practice and take it with you wherever you go. Never leave home, or be at home, without it. Stay present in the moment so that amidst all that comes your way, amidst the ten thousand things that surround you on a daily basis, your vision will be clear, clean, honest, and consistent with the essence of your inner self.

This will make a tremendous difference in your relationships. Many families and beautiful friendships have been unduly fractured by misinterpretations and colliding 'identities'. Keep in mind, you are also influenced by other people who are putting their 'self' together and sorting through the maze just like everyone else.

The many elements that have shaped you also include the love, good fortune, and incredible experiences you have been blessed with throughout the years; they are worthwhile and keepers to cherish. Others have no value and are only impediments on your path. Those you want to toss out. This will free up an incredible amount of energy. You just want to do a little house-cleaning. Pick and choose what parts you want to keep, and which ones you want to let go of. This is self-reflection, refining who you know yourself to be.

In doing so, you will feel healthier, lighter, and more comfortable in your own skin; your mind will be at peace. Otherwise, it is like trying to fit into a tailored shirt that no longer fits. The neck is too tight and the sleeves are too short and no matter how much you fidget and fudge and hope for the best, tugging on the cuffs to lengthen the sleeves is futile and nothing you do seems to work. The truth is, you have outgrown it. It is time for a new, comfortable shirt that fits and makes you happy.

Roles and identities are not a bad thing. They can be extremely healthy and valuable. They are a necessary and practical aspect of life and are essential for having a world that functions. We derive a great deal of fulfillment, love and satisfaction from the roles that we play, caring for our families and loved ones, serving others and contributing to society.

What is at the heart of the opportunity at hand, is to take a look at where you are today and where you want to go. Your identities were and are being created by you, and you can dismantle them any time you choose and create new ones. You might want to make a slight adjustment here and a little tweak there, that is perfect. Or, you might want to make a major turn-around, if so, go for it. Either way, this is your journey, and your meditation practice will support you every step of the way.

Present Moment Meditation
Everyday Tools and Practices
Chapter Five – Roles and Identities

MEDITATION – FREE FROM IDENTITIES

1. Follow steps 1-8 on page 21-22 (in Chapter One)

2. Relax your entire body. As you breathe in, let your awareness remain inside. Maintain inner awareness even as you exhale. Notice the space inside that fills your entire being, how it appears formless and encompasses every direction—in front and behind, above and below, to the sides and in every direction. Let this space expand. Notice, that regardless of how far you let it expand, it can continue going even further. There is no end as to how far it can reach. There are no parameters, boundaries, or limitations. It is infinite. Recognize that this boundless space is in fact, your inner self. It is completely free. You are completely free. Bask in this awareness.

3. Continue for at least ten minutes.

4. Before you open your eyes, notice how any identities that you have acquired, are separate from the boundless experience of the vast inner space. Nothing can limit or confine it, or the inner self. Notice how they are completely independent and free.

5. Take your time, and finish up.

6. Gently bring your awareness back to your body and back to the room, and slowly open your eyes. Take a few moments before resuming activity.

PRACTICE

1. As you go about your day, become aware of how many hats you wear, how many roles you play, and how many identities you have. There are so many! Notice which ones are in harmony with your awareness of self, and which ones conflict with your peace and contentment. Are there any identities that you would like to alter or let go of?

2. Become aware of how often you identify with your roles, such that you think who you are is in fact that role, and whether that mindset constricts or expands you. Does it give you more or less freedom? Are there ways you can create a shift so that any of your identities add more space and enjoyment to your life? Maintain the awareness that your essence is never bound by identities, it remains free.

The ways in which we interpret and perceive the nuances of who we are, our experience of our self from the inside out and the outside in, and the life around us, creates a multitude of dimensions that affect our happiness, peace of mind, self-esteem, self-worth, self-expression, and our ability to be comfortable in our own skin.

6

THE PRISM
OF
THE MIND

*When you speak kindly about
yourself you can feel it; it makes you
happy and content. It sends positive
vibes throughout your body, mind
and spirit. Other people appreciate it
and will be inclined to follow your
lead. It is a win-win.*

"The mind experiences only that which it contemplates, that which it itself constructs; the mind is nothing but what has been put together by thought. Knowing this, do as you please."
—Yoga Vasistha

There is another piece, *the* most critical component that we must take into consideration when discussing human beings and their desire for contentment and happiness. It is what the masters have discussed for thousands of years and is what shapes all of our experiences. In addition to knowing our inner self, it is the most important aspect of who we are as human beings and what we must understand if we want to be happy and at peace. Once we become aware of this and keep it in the scope of our daily practice, we are home free. And that one element is, the mind. It is through the prism of the mind that we interpret everything that happens, all of our experiences as well as how we feel about ourselves and the entirety of life. The mind is our best friend or our worst enemy. And that is why we meditate and practice self-awareness, to quiet the wandering activity of the mind.

How fascinating! How often do you think about your mind, your relationship to it, and the role that it plays in your life? Do you pay attention to your mind and its correlation to your happiness? Usually, we go about our day and the mind is there with us, in the foreground or the background, but always present. From the moment we wake up until we close our eyes to sleep, and sometimes even while we are sleeping, it is doing its thing—thinking, judging, comparing, worrying, interpreting, creating, dictating, talking about this and talking about that. It drifts into the past and travels into the future, but is rarely fully present in the moment. Sometimes its perceptions are positive and sometimes not so much. We follow its lead as if it is the end all be all, the head honcho. No more! It is time we take control and make it our absolute best friend as we live present in our life.

How do you relate to your mind? Don't we usually think that the activity of the mind is who we are? Yikes, no stability there as the mind's natural tendency is to be restless. Have you ever considered that your mind is a separate entity from who you know yourself to be? Have you ever considered that you and your mind are not one and the same? Exploring this further leads us to a new and critical dimension of knowing ourselves.

The mind thinks, *I am content,* so we believe that we are content. Fantastic, keep up the good work! The mind says, *I am unlovable,* so we believe that we are unlovable, which is based on the past and evidence that was created and believed. This way of thinking is not so fantastic and does not generate peace and harmony in your heart, soul or life, so change that thought immediately! Turn it around, say to yourself with full conviction and belief, *I am loveable.* This is how we take control of our mind. It is that simple. However, it requires constant awareness and discipline. We must remain aware of our mind at all times, especially when it takes us in a direction that leads us away from the inner self, in a direction that is contrary to the goal of our path. The mind is powerful, sly and tricky; it wants to have its way. If we do not remain awake to what is going on in the mind, we can end up in places that we never intended to go. Such is the power of the mind.

Have you ever driven for a few miles and then realized that you do not remember consciously choosing to turn onto those streets? That is because you were preoccupied, absorbed in another place in your mind, rather than being present to where you were driving. My students have shared that even while they are reading, in the background their mind is thinking about something else, unrelated to what they are reading. The mind is so powerful! Therefore, one of your primary practices must be to become aware of what is taking place in your mind.

When you take a few minutes during your day and become aware of your breathing, as you gently ride the wave of your in-breath and out-breath, the mind is stabilized and remains present in the moment. This is an easy way to train the mind as you go about your everyday activities. How amazing, that something as powerful as the mind can be retrained and held steady in the moment, simply by becoming aware of your breath.

Another practice relating to the mind is to become aware of its habits and tendencies; you want healthy mental habits that are consistent with living a peaceful, fulfilled life. Who would ever think that the mind has habits! Believe it or not, it does.

Let us say, at eleven o'clock at night just before going to bed, even though you are cutting back on eating late because you know it is unhealthy and affects the quality of your sleep, your mind, from previous conditioning says, "Let's have a midnight snack." Before you know it, you are sneaking around the kitchen peeking into the cupboards and opening the refrigerator door, and not long after are back on the couch munching away on your snack. All because of a single thought.

Some habits and tendencies of the mind have been around for a long time and go back as early as childhood. They are engrained internally and have become impressions, like the imprints that are left when a thumb is pressed into clay or silly putty. There are certain things that someone can say to you, or imply, and immediately you have a reaction; you have been there a million times before. Most often, these reactions are related to or are similar to something that has happened before; the scenario and the results are very predictable. The current situation might be new, but the source of the reaction is not. As soon as that earlier occurrence is triggered by what is now being said or done, in a millisecond your mind kicks into gear, makes the correlation, and you react. You are off and running, and unfortunately, it can be detrimental to your inner peace and tranquility.

One of my students is a lovely, middle-aged woman. During one of our conversations, she was telling me how content she was, and how proud she was of the life that she had put together. She liked where she lived, was at the height of her lifelong profession, and was healthy. And she had peace in her life, due to her commitment to her meditation practice.

The next time I saw her, she had just returned from an out-of-town family reunion where she had spent a few days with not-so-close relatives. She felt like an outsider. As she relayed her experience, she got more and more worked up and started comparing her life with the people she had just been with. From the outside, it appeared that they were more successful than she was and were more bonded in their relationships. She began doubting and second-guessing herself, which was an old habit—maybe she should have made different choices, maybe this, maybe that, escalating the intensity as she continued.

Her body demeanor changed as I looked into her eyes and watched her disappear further and further into some distant world in her mind that had just kidnapped her and now inhabited her body. A vortex was sucking the life right out of her. I started calling to her, "Come back, come back! You love your life, come back!" A few minutes later she rescued herself and rejoined the life that she loved and we had a good laugh. Phew, that was a close call! But that is how fast it can happen. Such is the power of the mind and our thoughts.

It is the nature of birds to fly, and it is the nature of the mind to think. The mind is fickle, restless, and rarely satisfied. It is the mind that creates our inner dialogue that shapes how and what we think about ourselves, others, our life, and the world—everything. The mind affects our ability to love and can interfere with our precious relationship with our inner self.

The activity of the mind is like clouds that block the light of the sun. When flying in an airplane on an overcast day, there is a point in the ascent when the plane breaks through the clouds and suddenly you are surrounded by blue sky and sunshine! The sun was there all the time, but you could not see it because the clouds blocked its light. Likewise, the self is always present; it is the activity of the mind that blocks its light.

Self-awareness and observing the mind, keeps its activity healthy and positive. Think good thoughts. The mind has tremendous power! People have been healed through the power of intentions and the mind. Mankind has achieved incredible feats due to the power of the mind. Astronauts have been launched into outer space! There is no limit to what the mind is capable of. It is a pure, clean, quiet mind that leads one to their inner self and a joy-filled life. A mind that is present in the moment is at peace. A mind that is at peace is present in the moment.

Present Moment Meditation
Everyday Tools and Practices
Chapter Six – The Prism of the Mind

MEDITATION – STEADINESS OF MIND

1. Follow steps 1-8 on page 21-22 (in Chapter One)

2. Relax your entire body. With your attention within, become aware of the inner stillness. As you do so, notice that in that stillness, is your self. The mind is quiet, yet even in the absence of thought, there is a sense of being, a knowing that you exist. Notice how this awareness of being is unrelated to any movement of the mind. Rather, it is pure consciousness, subtle yet present, completely free from any knowing that is associated with the mind. Your mind is at peace, it is resting in the love of the self.

3. Continue for at least ten minutes.

4. Before you open your eyes, as you transition out of meditation notice how thoughts begin to manifest. At first they are faint, and then gradually they become more present. While maintaining the tranquility of your meditation, watch the thoughts as they appear, noticing that they are separate from you. You and your thoughts are not one and the same; you remain unaffected by their movement, as you are established in inner peace.

5. Take your time, and finish up.

6. Gently bring your awareness back to your body and back to the room, and slowly open your eyes. Take a few moments before resuming activity.

PRACTICE

1. Throughout the day, become aware of your thoughts and your mind. Listen to what it is saying. Become aware of its habits and tendencies. Notice which mental patterns bring you contentment, and which ones are detrimental to your health, happiness, and well-being. Watch the movement of your mind, notice how it flits from here to there and then back again. Keep it steady by practicing breath awareness and staying present in the moment.

2. As soon as you notice any negative thoughts that do not lead you in an uplifting direction, immediately stop that thought and rephrase it in a positive way. This is just a habit and habits can be broken and new ones created. Training the mind and curbing its restless tendencies is a constant practice. Make your mind your friend, your helpful companion on your journey.

The sunlight shining through the stained glass window brings its magnificence to life. It gives it vibrancy, illuminating the images crafted by the artist. Without the light, the mosaic sleeps in darkness. The sunlight shines in full glory and never questions its value or doubts its luminosity.

7

THE PULL
OF THE
SENSES

*Everything in the physical realm
is constantly changing. Therefore, it
is unwise to look for lasting
happiness in the external world. The
inner self is where we find stability,
it is never disturbed by change or
the comings and goings of life.*

"Whatever inclination may arise, it is first awakened in the mind. Whenever there is any impulse in the mind, it is expressed through the channel of the senses. The more the outward discipline is established, the greater the happiness."

—Jnaneshwari

High in the plateau meadows of the Himalayan mountains lives a deer known as the, musk deer. What makes this deer so special is that inside its belly near the navel region, is a gland that produces a beautiful, fragrant oil called, musk.

As the deer roams throughout the forest, he smells the musk and is captivated by its fragrance. He searches here and there, running, leaping, hunting, desperate to find the origin of the fragrant aroma. The faster he travels the more abundant the scent, and with persistent determination the deer's quest for the source of the musk continues.

Eventually, overcome by exhaustion and unsuccessful in his pursuit, the deer wears himself out and collapses. As he falls to the ground, his head lands upon his belly, and breathing in the enchanting scent of the musk, he realizes that the source of the fragrance that he was so desperately seeking in the forest around him, came from within himself.

This is a story from a long time ago that the masters used to illustrate the human predicament. In such a simple yet descriptive way, it portrays the one fundamental mistake that we make in our pursuit of happiness. And that is, we look outside of ourselves for joy, love, and fulfillment, when actually, the source of these, is within. As I look back and reflect upon my life, I can see time and time again how I mistakenly looked in the wrong direction.

The world and all its splendor is an incredible place to live. We see the beautiful blue sky and white puffy clouds, crimson autumn sunsets and starry midnight skies. All around us, we enjoy the many pleasures that life has to offer, as our five senses—sight, taste, smell, hearing and touch—are drawn outward, externally engaging in the world.

It is through the senses that we have a direct experience of life; they are the link between the outer world, and that which we experience so intimately within ourselves. We enjoy beautiful music and fine cuisine, the scent of a rose, the face of a loved one, and the tender touch of a newborn. Without the sense of taste, honey would just be honey, there would not be much of an experience beyond that. Our senses are so deeply woven into our experience of being, that we think that what we experience through them, *is* who we are.

The role of the senses is not something that we often think about; they are taken for granted as part and parcel of who we are. Yet, they play a powerful role as we discover our true nature.

It is the mind working in conjunction with the senses, that creates our experiences. The mind gives reality to the senses as it interprets that which we see, hear, taste, smell, and touch, and in the process of interpreting, adds meaning. It is the mind that identifies, categorizes, and distinguishes between that which we like and that which we do not, that which we want more of and that which we want less of. This push and pull, this 'more of' and 'less of' exchange is a constant interplay that goes on all day long, and has been since infancy.

Although this can be exhausting and an easy way to lose touch with our inner self, overall there is not anything wrong with it. We are meant to enjoy and employ the senses, as they add color, texture, and dimension to life. However, there is one inherent problem, a rather big problem. And that is when we mistakenly think that the joy we experience through the senses comes from the objects that we see, hear, taste, smell, and touch. We think that the pleasure we experience from eating a yummy piece of cake, comes from the cake; that the joy of looking at a painting, comes from the painting. And although the cake was yummy and the painting was beautiful, the joy was not in the cake itself, it was inside you. It is so easy to forget this, and so easy to think that the joy came from the outside object.

In the same way that our thoughts take on a reality of their own, so does our experience of the senses. It is through the powerful pull of the senses that we seek pleasure, the outward pursuit of looking for 'something' that will fill us up and make us whole. We search for more of that which we think is the source of our happiness, however, this is counterproductive as this kind of happiness is only temporary.

Gratification of the senses is also used to indulge, suppress, avoid and numb, sometimes to the point where it becomes excessive. No doubt, this will not bring lasting happiness. It is detrimental to the body, mind and spirit, and is an obstacle on the path of self-discovery. One of my students shared, "I see that it's more important to fill me up from inside, rather than fill my time trying to fill me up from outside."

The senses play a key role in keeping the dance of life in motion. However, self-control, one of the gatekeepers, is essential for maintaining health and harmony on a daily basis. And so is meditating. When we meditate, we quiet the senses and redirect their outward tendencies; we gently turn them inward. This seems so simple, yet it is very powerful and healing. Managing the senses can bring balance to every aspect of life. Then we will enjoy true happiness.

In the early 1980s, I was living at a meditation center in India. It was lunchtime and I was sitting on the floor of the huge dining hall with maybe one hundred other people. We sat cross-legged, side-by-side, in long rows with an aisle in-between, large enough for the servers to pass by and ladle the rice and vegetable dishes onto our round, stainless steel trays. There were rules that we were asked to abide by, such as no talking during meals. It created an atmosphere of respect for the food, as well as being able to eat it in a calm environment. That was no problem, I enjoyed doing that.

One afternoon just after I had been served, I was suddenly overcome with an overflowing feeling of joy that filled me up like I had never experienced before. I started laughing and could not stop. For forty-five minutes I tried to eat and be discreet and respect the silence rules but all I could do was laugh. I was never able to finish my meal. It was a telling experience, showing me that beyond a doubt that the uncontainable delight that bubbled up inside like a giant fountain arose on its own without any outside stimulus. My self was unleashing its infinite joy. And to think, even when I am not experiencing it, this quality of joy is always present within me.

Present Moment Meditation
Everyday Tools and Practices
Chapter Seven – The Pull of the Senses

MEDITATION – THE TREASURE IS WITHIN

1. Follow steps 1-8 on page 21-22 (in Chapter One)

2. Relax your entire body. As you breathe in, imagine that your mind melts into your breath, let the two become one, and then exhale. Repeat for two to three rounds of breathing, going deeper within with every in-breath. Now, relax your ears, and the sense of hearing. Relax your nose, and the sense of smell. Relax your tongue, and the sense of taste. Relax your eyes, and the sense of sight. Relax your skin, and the sense of touch. With the body, mind and senses quiet, be with that which remains, the energy of love and contentment in the center of your being.

3. Continue for at least ten minutes.

4. Before you open your eyes, notice how much more relaxed your entire being is, when the senses are quiet and given an opportunity to rest. Notice too, that when the senses are quiet, you are able to go deeper into meditation and better able to connect with your inner self.

5. Take your time, and finish up.

6. Gently bring your awareness back to your body and back to the room, and slowly open your eyes. Take a few moments before resuming activity.

PRACTICE

1. As you enjoy life and the many opportunities that are available to engage your senses, take note of the relationship between you, your senses, your mind, and the object of the senses, that which fulfills them. What is your relationship with this interplay? Are you aware that the joy that you are experiencing is coming from within you, or do you think that it is from the objects enjoyed by the senses? Watch, and see what you notice.

2. Moderation is so important! Too much of anything creates imbalance, agitates the mind, and makes it harder to stay connected with your self. So practice moderation and be mindful of the choices that you make.

We search and search, looking for our eye glasses. We dig deep into pockets and rummage through drawers. We check under the seats and empty our purse. All the while, they are on top of our head, right where we put them. They were never lost. In the same way, we search for the self, but it was never lost. It has always been there, inside. It was there all the time.

<u>8</u>

KNOWING
THE
PURE, I AM

Consciousness is everywhere, and is known by many names. It is called the Self, Spirit, Soul, Universal Energy, Awareness, and more. It doesn't matter what you call it. If you would like, you can refer to it by your own name.

"Ask yourself: In the absence of my desires and thoughts, who or what am I? Reflection of this sort is a yearning of the soul, which we all have at some time or other, to recognize our true identity, I Am."
—Swami Satyasangananda

About fifteen years ago, I participated in a personal growth seminar along with ninety other participants. The course leader was a woman from San Francisco who was in her late-sixties and had the vitality of a thirty-year old. I immediately liked her; she was dynamic, self-assured, and masterful at her craft.

Chairs were arranged with theater seating; a half-moon shape with two side aisles and a main aisle in the center of the room. My chair was the first one off the center aisle near the front. While delivering the content of the class, she often stood just a few feet away from where I was sitting. I studied her every move.

If participants wanted to share or ask a question, we were supposed to raise our hand. But one moment got the better of me. She was standing near me while I listened with rapt attention. As she paused to take a breath I said aloud, "I want to be just like you!" Her co-leader quickly came forward from the back of the room, stood at the edge of my chair and looked me straight in the eyes and said, "You'll be her when you be you." What a cool thing to say!

I have thought about this many times since. When I am confident and comfortable with myself, I am imbibing those qualities that I recognized and respected in her. And, when I am not comfortable with myself, I look to see what there is for me to let go of or what kind of shift I want to make. Remember, nothing is ever added to who we are, as we are already whole and complete. We can only remove what is blocking our inner light; and then that which we are *not* falls away, and as a result, ..."you will be you."

Wanting to 'find myself' or 'know who I am' can also be a profound endeavor. In fact, according to the meditation masters, asking the question, *Who Am I?* is the most important question that a human being can ask. They say that only by exploring deeper into this meaningful question can a person understand and know who they are. The circumstances that bring the search of self to light can vary. Sometimes they are relevant and other times, not so much. But that is not important. What really matters is that we arrive at the doorstep of self-inquiry and contemplate, *Who Am I?*

When describing the inner self, the masters say over and over again, that it is a pure state of being, that its essence is simply, *I Am*. What you might notice here, is that there are no adjectives, adverbs or modifiers that follow, *I Am*. It does not say, *"I am Kathleen, I am my body,*

I am tall, I am short, I am successful, I am unsuccessful." It simply declares, *I Am.* The best time to experience this is in meditation, in those moments when you find yourself in a deep state of quiet equilibrium, when the body, mind and senses are quiet. In the absence of activity, in the tranquil interior space, there is no effort or angst, you are just being. There is a feeling that arises, a distinct knowing of, *I Am, I exist.*

Whenever you add anything to your declarations of, *I Am,* that are not consistent with the qualities of the self—peaceful, loving, fulfilled—you have qualified and quantified it, and your *I Am* experience is no longer that of the unchanging self. Instead, your *I Am* experience exists in the world of duality, where judgments, limitations and comparisons prevail. In that world, everything is relative—more of this, and less of that. If you apply these examples to yourself, *"I am enough of this, but I am not enough of that,"* or similar statements, there is instability because your experiences are always changing. *"I am happy today, but I am not quite as happy as I was yesterday, which was more than the day before, yet not as happy as I am hoping to be tomorrow..."* When discussing this topic in class, one of my longtime students shared, "Anything that is fleeting is not me."

It is amazing how many times this habitual tendency occurs on any given day, as we juxtapose ourselves against the world of the ten thousand things, the conversations in our head, and our emotions. That is just the way human beings are wired. However, by staying present in the moment, by remaining aware of these types of patterns, they can be reshaped and transformed into something uplifting and wonderful. With regular practice, they can change the ambiance of your day and your life. Try these on: *"I am blessed," "I am grateful,"* and one that was shared by another student, *"I am enough."*

For about twenty years, a group of ten friends that included my husband and I, would alternate hosting potluck dinner parties. Sometimes they would be in the summer, but mostly they were in December during the holidays. One year, we were hosting at our home, and I was providing the entree. I was thrilled to be serving our dear friends one of my specialty dishes—delicious salmon patties made with celery and onions and a pinch of fresh thyme. They were baked in muffin tins, so when served, they were shaped like muffin cakes. So cute! Martha Stewart would have been proud of me. They were accompanied by fresh mashed potatoes and homemade vegetarian gravy that was out of this world.

So, there we all were, seated at the table with candlelight and cloth napkins, reminiscing and enjoying each other with stories and laughter. Except—we were halfway through the meal and the topic of conversation kept reverting back to how fabulous the pecan appetizer salad was that one of the guests had brought. There was absolutely no mention of my adorable salmon muffins sitting in the middle of their plates. I kept waiting, and waiting, wearing a hostess smile, meanwhile, my heart rate was increasing by the minute and the muscles in my throat were tightening up. I was afraid to open my mouth in fear of what I might say. *"Can someone pleeease acknowledge the salmon cakes?!"* Sitting at the end of the table, I watched the whole scenario playing out inside of me. I recognized what was happening, but there was little I could do to snap out of it; it had a hold on me. In that moment, I was a salmon patty!

When you are connected to the unadulterated state of, *I Am*, you will know by the way you feel. When your heart is happy, you are in that state. When you are being generous and kind and giving without expectations or keeping score, you are in that state. When you genuinely give love to yourself and others, there is a comfortable feeling and you are at ease, because love is your natural state of being.

Paramahansa Yogananda was a great teacher from India who brought meditation to America in the 1920s. He passed away in 1952 and is still considered to be one of the most influential meditation teachers worldwide. He once said that when we experience anger or greed, say to yourself, *"That is not me."* And, when you experience love and gratitude, say to yourself, *"That is me!"* When you feel a spring in your step and connected to the world, say, *"That is me!"* When you are proud of yourself for a job well done, recognize, *"That is me!"* When you go the extra mile to help someone, declare, *"That is me!"*

Noticing the thoughts that you entertain and the way you talk to and about yourself, either aloud or privately, is a powerful self-awareness tool that can easily be practiced. When you catch yourself saying, "I am _____," if it is self-defeating or not in alignment with your vision for yourself, immediately change it to a phrase that is positive and uplifting. Your experience of yourself and your life will quickly change for the better!

Extraordinary and lofty words have been used by meditation masters to describe the inner self. They refer to it as consciousness, saying that it is the same cosmic awareness that exists everywhere in the universe. That is why, when we are kind, generous, forgiving, and compassionate we feel connected to each other, because the same consciousness that is in you, is in me.

They say that the self is infinite, and that experiencing it is so sublime that there are no words to describe it. The best portrayal they have found is that it is a state of unending bliss. They also say that it is eternal; it is never born and never dies. This can be difficult to comprehend through the mind; something that is never born and never dies is a rare concept indeed.

I once went to a nearby church where an elderly monk from Asia was giving a talk. It was a very intimate room, so I was able to sit close to the front where he was sitting. He had the most peaceful, gentle, happy face I have ever seen. I aspire to have that kind of look on my face, because if my face looks that peaceful, I will also be very peaceful inside. Peace like that cannot be ruffled.

The attendees were given the opportunity to ask him questions, so I thought, this is my chance. I wrote my question on an index card: *How can the self have no beginning and no end? Doesn't everything have a beginning and an end?*

Even though he did not know me, and there was no indication that it was my question, he looked directly at me, smiled and said, "It has a beginning, we just haven't found it yet!" Then he added, "Look inside your own meditation, look for it there, find it there."

Present Moment Meditation
Everyday Tools and Practices
Chapter Eight – Knowing the Pure, I Am

MEDITATION – THE PURE, I AM

1.   Follow steps 1-8 on page 21-22 (in Chapter One)

2.   Relax your entire body. As you breathe in, let your whole being, every pore and every cell of your body, mind and senses, fill with the awareness of the pure, *I Am*. Breathing in, silently repeat, *"I"*, and as you exhale silently repeat, *"Am."* Repeat for at least seven rounds of breathing. Then, in this pure state of *I Am*, take the vantage point of an observer, an impartial witness, and simply observe. Remain detached, as if your inner light of consciousness shines in every direction like the radiant light of the sun.

3.   Continue for at least ten minutes.

4.   Before you open your eyes, recognize that the experience of this pure state of being is taking place within you. It is you. Its radiance is your essence. Its love is your essence. Its purity and the experience of being whole and complete is your essence. Enjoy the immense freedom that is inherent in the witness point-of-view. Savor this experience.

5.   Take your time, and finish up.

6. Gently bring your awareness back to your body and back to the room, and slowly open your eyes. Take a few moments before resuming activity.

PRACTICE

1. Become aware of everything—adjectives, adverbs, or any type of qualifying statements or opinions—that you add to the pure, *I Am*. Listen to what you say to and about yourself, either privately or aloud. Words are powerful; your thoughts create your experience of yourself. Throughout the day, silently repeat, *"I Am."* It makes a big difference and will keep you centered.

2. While going about your day, regardless of how hectic it might be, create the experience inwardly of simply *being*. Even if you are running from one commitment to the next, inwardly, remain steady. Find that which is 'constant' within you. Let this mindset be the ambiance of your day, whether it is in the foreground or the background. Find stillness, even in the midst of activity.

When your worldly cares are suspended, regardless of how long or short it lasts, the time spent with your self is not only life changing, it is validating. It confirms that there is more to you than what the eyes can see. It confirms that there is, inside, a permanent sense of self.

9

GRATITUDE
AND
CONTENTMENT

*Each time I close my eyes
and turn my attention inward to
that quiet place inside myself, my
experience of love grows; and as
that love gently blossoms, so too
do patience, kindness, generosity,
gratitude, and contentment.*

"As long as one is not satisfied in the inner self, he will be subjected to unhappiness. With the rise of contentment, the purity of one's heart blooms. The contented man who possesses nothing owns the world."

—Yoga Vasistha

Contentment, one of the four gatekeepers, is perhaps the greatest of all. It is the leader of the pack. When contentment is present, so are all of the other gems—love, compassion, gratitude, ease and comfort, peace of mind, generosity and all of the qualities that nurture the soul and add richness to life. Where there is love, there is contentment. Where there is happiness, there is contentment. When we are content, we are fulfilled.

A few years ago, my husband and I were hosting out-of-town company at our home. It had been a long time since we had upgraded some of our décor, so we thought this would be a good time to take on that project. Decorating is not necessarily my forte; I am not bad at it but I am not high end either. Our home is comfortable.

The furniture in the living room was hodge-podge; a small white wicker table given to me by my mother was at the end of the couch. A thirty-inch high ceramic Roman pedestal with a round glass top from Michael's was used as a telephone stand. We definitely needed a new couch. When sitting on the cushions, you would practically sink to the floor.

In 1993, we had purchased a television from Sears Roebuck using the eight-hundred dollars that I had just won on a Wheel of Fortune slot machine at a nearby casino. I somewhat redeemed myself from my earlier Wheel of Fortune debacle! We were thrilled when we bought the new television since it was a lot bigger than the twelve-by-nine inch tiny version we were currently using that was so small we had to squint to see the picture.

Anyway, the Sears television still worked fine so I did not see any reason to put money into replacing it with a more up-to-date flat-screen version. It was the kind of television that was so deep and big and bulky that no one wanted them even for free, nor could they be put out to the curb on trash day because they were so heavy, no one could pick them up.

My cousin came over to give me decorating ideas; her face said it all. She perused the room then said, "The first thing you need to do is get rid of that TV."

So we did. We waited in the long line behind SUVs and pick-up trucks at our city's hazardous waste recycling day, along with the rest of our community who were upgrading and making the switch. We were definitely not alone; it was unbelievable how many of those humungous televisions were still out there.

When we started the re-do project, we decided together which items we would keep, which ones would be tossed out or given away, and what we would buy new, working within our allotted budget. At one point when I was probably getting a little bit anxious, wanting everything to be 'perfect' Bob said, "We'll work with what we have."

I loved that. It was so helpful at the time, and has been ever since. It gave me such ease and comfort. I could relax and enjoy what we were doing and be content and grateful for all that we had.

You can create contentment any time you would like. It is a powerful ally. Sometimes, it is already present, naturally there on its own. You did not have to do anything to bring it forth. At other times, contentment does not feel close at all, for instance, when you are struggling, upset, or anxious. But even then, contentment is not far away. You can manifest it on your own; you can fill your entire being with contentment. It is so easy to do and only takes a few moments, and has an incredibly calming effect.

Wherever you are, no matter what you are doing (not while driving or operating machinery), or regardless of your current state of mind, you can create contentment. All you have to do is become aware of your breathing. As you inhale, imagine that you are filling your entire body, mind, and spirit with the velvety richness of contentment.

Let this feeling expand throughout every pore of your being, so much so that your body cannot contain it and it shines way beyond your physical body into the space around you, and even further out into the world. Let its soothing power heal, relax, and restore you. You can also incorporate this practice as you begin or transition out of your meditation.

During one of my classes we were discussing contentment, and each student had an opportunity to share their thoughts, experiences, and insights. One woman who was a regular attendee shared, *"I am already content."* WOW! That is so powerful! There are many golden nuggets in this phrase, let us take a closer look.

If you say, *"I am already content,"* it is being spoken in the present tense. Therefore, when you repeat it, you are creating that in *this present moment*, you are content. That is a potent declaration to say to yourself! Notice also, that it relates to the pure awareness of, *I Am*, and that it is consistent with the qualities of the self, as the self is always content. Also, by stating, *I am already content*, it implies that that is who you were before and who you are now, that it is your indisputable essence and whether or not more or less of anything is added or subtracted it does not matter because you are already content.

I absolutely love this mantra and have used it regularly ever since that day when it was shared in class. Sometimes, I say it silently to myself just because it makes me happy and grateful. And other times—when I compare myself to others or think that something is lacking or should be other than it is—when the waves are rough and I am trying to stay afloat and keep my nose above water, this mantra is my savior and trusted companion. It anchors me and prevents me from getting swept away in a current that could otherwise drag me in a direction where I do not want to go. *"I am already content,"* reminds me of who I am, the beauty in my life, that I am whole and complete, and that I am blessed.

When experiencing contentment, there is one more thing that you can include, and that is, gratitude. Gratitude and contentment are practically twins, barely inseparable. When you are content, it is also natural to be grateful. Decide right now, to make it a habit to become aware of gratitude and contentment. You will feel abundant, regardless of how much or how little you have in your life. One drop of contentment, one drop of gratitude, goes a long, long way. You can incorporate this practice as a regular part of your day. Invite others to participate with you.

I have found that being aware of gratitude and contentment on a daily basis keeps me present in the moment, and keeps me connected to my heart center, the place of love within myself. Gratitude and contentment are grounding forces and great supports, regardless of what is going on. They are indisputable pillars of strength. When I am grateful and content, I know that *I am enough* and that I have what it takes to surmount any challenges that come my way. Contentment includes the awareness that nothing is lacking. It means that everything is as it should be, even when it does not appear to be. When I am content, I am more accepting of others and tremendously grateful for everyone and everything in my life.

I have spoken very highly, and proudly, about my students throughout this book. Now, you can hear directly from some of them in their own words! I asked them to share a few words about, "What does contentment mean to you?" Here are their replies. Enjoy!

"Contentment is accepting what is. Contentment is experiencing gratitude and being aware of the peace within." — CM

"Contentment is an appreciation for what you have and, more importantly, who you are. Contentment promotes serenity, tolerance for yourself and others, empathy and peace." — BC

"Contentment, to me, means peace in my life. Peace is present when negativity and anger are absent. It is being satisfied and grateful for all I have and leaves no desire for more 'stuff.' Living in the present moment and accepting myself as I am, is the key to my contentment." — SW

"Contentment to me means saying, "Yes" to life, even the hard parts—not needing to be free of discomfort and fear. It is complete acceptance and non-judgment of people and circumstances." — JK

"When I think of contentment, I compare it to happiness. Contentment surpasses happiness because it is not fleeting; it is long-lasting and embodies gratitude. Also, I remember during one of our classes we pondered the difference between happiness and contentment. Over time, I began to clearly see the difference, whereas previously, I thought they were one in the same. I now strive to be content." — JC

"Contentment to me means lacking nothing. It means feeling satisfied and peaceful. It helps me come from a place of giving, because I have more than I need." — LB

"Contentment is a feeling of my soul settling gently down. I don't want to do anything more or be anywhere else. The sights, sounds, light, and air are vivid. Time slows down and all is as it should be—there is no wanting—just being." — KS

"Contentment to me means a feeling deep inside that says, "Everything is all right, everything is as it should be." It means that I am at ease with my observation of the present moment. It has to do with equanimity, a steadiness within, regardless of the outside world." — MWL

"Contentment is seeing beauty in the 'everyday'. It is being free from excess worry and fear. It means being happy despite imperfections of life, and effortlessly living with ease." — DP

"Contentment means accepting whatever happens. I am content when my family is healthy and happy." — JG

"Contentment means being satisfied, at peace, and loving thyself. Our mental, physical, and spiritual journey is healed by having a spirit of contentment." — CT

"Contentment to me means being happy with what I am and have, and accepting and being ok with things that I cannot change." — RM

"A contented soul is one that flows with, not against, the stream of life. They make lemonade when necessary. This soul habitually searches for positive thoughts, and remains non-judgmental. His core is a pillar of gratitude for all that he has, and he never harbors jealousy." — KR

"Daily meditation, prayer, and inner silence help me achieve contentment with myself and others, and draws me closer to God." — MC

"Contentment is a goal of mine on a daily basis. I achieve it by practicing acceptance, surrender, and of course, meditation." — MZ

Present Moment Meditation
Everyday Tools and Practices
Chapter Nine – Gratitude and Contentment

MEDITATION – I AM GRATEFUL, I AM CONTENT

1. Follow steps 1-8 on page 21-22 (in Chapter One)

2. Relax your entire body. Breathe in, and breathe out. With every inhalation, fill your whole being with contentment. Notice that this experience of contentment contains perfect harmony and equilibrium. Now, as you inhale, silently say, *"Breathing in, I am grateful,"* and as you exhale say, *"Breathing out, I am content."* Continue repeating this mantra with your breath for at least seven rounds of breathing. Recognize that contentment is your natural state. Become so filled with contentment that your body cannot contain it, and this feeling expands into the space that surrounds you.

3. Continue for at least ten minutes.

4. Before you open your eyes, become aware of the velvety richness that is present when you experience contentment, and how you naturally settle into yourself. You are comfortable with yourself. Now, savor the sweetness of gratitude, and the natural quality of abundance that accompanies it.

5. Take your time, and finish up.

6. Gently bring your awareness back to your body and back to the room, and slowly open your eyes. Take a few moments before resuming activity.

PRACTICE

1. As you go about your day, take moments to call forth contentment. Notice the difference that it makes, the essence of calm, patience and acceptance that accompanies it. Also, express gratitude, silently or aloud, throughout your day. Notice how gratitude and contentment add a quality of balance within yourself and in your life.

2. When you start your day, think of three things that you are grateful for. Throughout your day, say, "Thank you" three times to someone. As you end your day, think of three things that you are grateful for.

Gratitude and contentment come from within. We know this to be true because we have experienced it many times. There is a peaceful quality, radiant and pure, like the stillness in a pond that reflects the light of the moon. Gratitude and contentment spontaneously arise when we walk in nature or sit beside a gentle stream. They are present when we count the many blessings in our life.

10

YOU
ARE
INVITED

The subtle heart is a formless, intimately comfortable space of love at the center of our being. While resting there in meditation, the energy of the heart transforms who we know ourselves to be; we experience who we are as love.

"Don't look back, look forward with infinite energy, infinite enthusiasm, infinite daring, and infinite patience—then alone can great deeds be accomplished. Tell your body that it is strong, tell your mind that it is strong, and have unbounded faith in yourself."
                                        —Swami Vivekananda

Back in the 1980s, I bought a really cool puzzle that was a fantastical image of a peacock, yet after all these years, I had never assembled it. Flash forward to 2019, when I thought putting the puzzle together would be a fun project for Bob and I to do over the Christmas and New Year holidays. The border of the puzzle did not have straight edges like most puzzles. Instead, it was in the shape of a peacock, outlining the feet, breast and fanned plumage of majestic feathers. And within the peacock, were pictures within pictures—two snakes, a seahorse, a fish, two cats—as well as colorful paisley swirls, stripes and polka dots. It was one-thousand pieces and very difficult to do. It took us, well, mostly Bob, until mid-March to complete it.

There is something very gratifying about looking at the many possible shapes spread out on the table, and finding the precise piece, the only piece, that perfectly fits into the spot. SNAP! A snug fit; there is no second-guessing.

What I like about puzzles, is the 'snap', when the piece that was chosen from the hundreds of other possibilities, is the exact one that further unifies all the other pieces and helps complete the overall image of the puzzle.

The invitation of *A Journey of Self-Discovery* embraces a wide panorama of opportunities, including taking a look at who you are beyond your name, form, persona, and the many roles that you have played throughout your lifetime. It is an invitation to take a look and see what might be missing in your life, a piece that once found, fits perfectly with your vision for yourself; a piece that enhances your joy and contentment and supports you on your path.

Or, maybe there is something, either internally or externally, that you would like to let go of so that it no longer bogs you down. By letting go, other pieces of your life will now fit harmoniously together.

Perhaps you prefer to let life naturally unfold. You will wait and see what presents itself as an opportunity, trusting that when it appears, you will recognize it and know that it is the perfect piece that will enrich your life.

You may want to adapt all three approaches, and that is fine. There are no rules; try things on and see what fits. Soften the parameters of your vision. Think outside the box so that new horizons open up, making room for fresh insights. The way you design your journey is completely up to you. That is the fun part and what makes the journey so special. It is an individual creation.

Today, at this stage of life, at any stage of life, it is good to know where you are going and how you are going to get there. What is your vision? What are your intentions? What do you want to create for yourself? What is the vehicle that will transport you? What aids and tools will support you along the way?

As you begin, it might seem as if a tiny spark awakens. Or a little voice whispers to you, but not necessarily in words. There is a familiar feeling that recognizes that what you are considering, or have an inkling of, is beneficial for you. It is as if a light goes on without you having flipped a switch. What is most important is that you begin.

There are so many opportunities to practice, and so many tools to choose from; all are user-friendly and they all work! They all lead you to your self, to a peaceful mind and a contented heart. Whether you choose a couple of tools or many, meditation is the key practice. And nothing goes to waste; everything that you do to nurture your path is a gateway to transformation and living an awakened life. It is an incredible process to experience and an awesome unfolding to observe. I cannot imagine my life without it.

The subtle heart center, which is the source of love, is also the home of the self. The masters say that although the self is everywhere, most specifically in a human being, it resides in the heart center. This heart has a voice, and if we listen very carefully, we can hear what it is saying. It requires very good listening skills, because its words can easily be drowned out by internal and external noise.

Refining my ability to hear the voice of my heart has become one of my primary practices in the last few years. It has been life-changing. I absolutely love and cherish this relationship. It has become my new best friend. I trust it implicitly, with no reserve or conditions.

When I was in the early stages of trusting the guidance of this voice, I found myself in a bit of a pickle. I so badly wanted to pick up the phone and communicate to a particular individual what I thought about the poor customer service that I had just received from their staff, which up to that point had been fine for the last two years. But my heart said, *No*, do not call. And boy, did I want to call. Every reactionary bone in my body wanted to pick up the phone and let them know, but no matter how much I practiced saying what I wanted to say, I could never find the words to communicate in a way that would not be damaging or unproductive. And I did not want that. So, I followed my heart and never called.

I am glad that I listened to my heart and followed its advice. That incident rooted me very deeply in trusting that relationship, and it has been there guiding me ever since. I rarely question it and if I do, it is only momentary. Otherwise, the risk is too great, as my peace of mind and happiness are at stake. Following its lead saves me a lot of aggravation and drama.

If the voice of your heart speaks to you, encouraging you to explore your inner self, trust that voice. If you sense that turning inward and meditating has value for you, trust that feeling. That which is drawing you nearer could be the very thing that knows what is best for you. It is calling you. Pay attention to what resonates with your center of love. The resonance of the heart is always true, and always in tune.

Let your heart guide you. If you make a choice that brings you joy, then it was a wise choice and an indication that you are in sync with your heart. Be attentive to your thoughts; make sure they resonate with your heart. If your heart says, "Don't go there," either literally or figuratively, then don't go there. If it tells you to grab a sweater before you run out the door, grab a sweater. One of my students said, "That voice is always right."

The path of self-discovery requires regular attention, nourishment and care, just as a tiny seed needs sunlight and water to flourish and grow. If it is neglected, it cannot bear fruit, and the nectar is in the fruit.

Self-effort and gentleness are 'must have' companions. Self-effort is the energy that keeps the journey alive. It maintains momentum as you continue moving forward. It is the fuel that keeps the engine running. Gentleness is the gift of compassion when doubts, obstacles, and setbacks arise. Gentleness is there to offer understanding and give you access to new perspectives.

For many years after leaving India and living in meditation centers, I would wake-up in the morning and one of my first thoughts would be, "Maybe today I'll become enlightened. Maybe today I'll see the Oneness of all creation and experience cosmic consciousness. Maybe today I'll lose myself in divine awareness." I would look into the eyes of the numerous pictures of sages and holy persons hanging on the walls in my meditation room and pray, "Please, let today be the day—"

And then one day, standing amidst the saintly faces surrounding me, I realized that although my aspirations were laudable, perhaps my 'hopefully today' mindset was inappropriate, fruitless, and quite frankly, ridiculous. This approach was not only the antithesis of what this journey is all about, it also discounted all that was available to me on that day, in the here and now. The faces of my holy pals made me happy; I trusted them, revered their guidance, and was immensely grateful for all that they had taught me. But I needed to create a shift in my outlook; I needed to get present in my life.

Even if I did not see scintillating white lights beaming from the hearts of humanity, what was best for me was to see the magic and splendor that was available to me at that stage of my journey and embrace that I was exactly where I was supposed to be. I needed to get present for real, not under the pretense of, "Hopefully today—"

And even if there was something more to attain, right then all that was required was for me to continue my practice with my two feet firmly on the ground, stepping forward in my life, one hundred percent, whether I merged with cosmic consciousness today, or not. That was not up to me anyway; my job was to continue my practice and let everything else unfold as it was meant to be.

So, the pictures came down and have been safely tucked away in a closet ever since. The writings of the masters continue to be a mainstay in my life. They remind me where it is that I am headed and the best way to get there. Their wisdom is nourishment for the growth of my soul and my journey. Their teachings transport me to a deeper level of knowing my self, and who we all are. Their compassionate and poignant words remind me of how to live among the world, without losing myself in it.

Present Moment Meditation
Everyday Tools and Practices

Chapter Ten – You Are Invited

MEDITATION – THE HEART CENTER

1. Follow steps 1-8 on page 21-22 (in Chapter One)

2. Relax your entire body. Bring your attention to your in-breath and follow it inside to the center of your chest, at the level of your heart. Keep your attention there. This very special place is the energy of the heart center, the source of love. Keep going deeper. This is a great place to reside during your meditation. Let the love in your heart grow, and shine in every direction. As you experience this love, recognize that it is coming from inside you, it is you.

3. Continue for at least ten minutes.

4. Before you open your eyes, while remaining in the energy of the heart center, bless your future. Bless all that is to come and the magnificent transformations that will unfold as you travel forward on your journey of self-discovery. Bless all of your future opportunities, intentions, and the many possibilities that await you.

5. Take your time, and finish up.

6. Gently bring your awareness back to your body and back to the room, and slowly open your eyes. Take a few moments before resuming activity.

PRACTICE

1. Throughout your day, check in with your heart center. Keep your intentions, thoughts, words and actions in harmony with the energy of your heart. Let it be your guide. Listen to it, trust it, and connect with it in meditation.

2. Set up your place for meditation, and meditate! Do as much as you can to support your practice. Find a good time to meditate, and make it a habit. Enjoy your meditations and acknowledge all that you gain from them. Incorporate the Present Moment Meditation Tools into your daily life; they are so easy to use and make such a difference. Keep up the good work!

Wrapped in the serenity of dawn's early light, in a quiet inlet harbor, a sailor unties the last rope that secures his boat to the dock. In the pivotal moment when the final knot releases, he is no longer bound to the shore, but instead, is free to set sail across the open water.

Thank you for joining me on this heartfelt, meaningful journey. I am excited for you and all that is yet to come; all that you will discover in the years, in the days, and in every present moment of your life.

Wishing you all the best, and peaceful meditations.   — *Kathleen*

Kathleen Henning was living in Hollywood, California in 1976, when she had an experience that would forever change her life. As she stood at the window of her apartment, she was overcome with a powerful feeling from deep within. She found herself asking, "Why am I here?"

When she heard about meditation and the inner journey, she recognized that this was the knowledge she was seeking. For the next six years, Kathleen lived full-time in meditation centers in India and the United States, immersing herself in study, meditation, and the journey of self-discovery.

In 2007, she founded Present Moment Meditation, a culmination of over 45 years of experience, and now leads classes on inner awareness and mastery of self. Her practical and light-hearted approach makes meditation inviting and beneficial for everyone. Her simple tools can easily be applied to everyday living, enriching every aspect of one's life.

Kathleen's relaxed style puts participants at ease, creating the perfect setting for transformations to occur. Sharing her insights, she guides others on their own journey of self-discovery. She released a CD, *Living in the Present Moment: Everyday Tools & Practices.*

Living in the Present Moment: Everyday Tools & Practices is a rich blend of beautiful music and soothing vocals exquisitely woven together for a complete body, mind and spirit experience of the present moment. It is peaceful, meditative, and a  great way to relax and unwind. It guides you through simple steps that enable you to center yourself and truly become 'quiet inside'.

The tools presented on this CD are simple, uplifting, and can easily be applied to everyday living. Practicing them throughout the day maintains peace of mind, increases happiness and well-being, and keeps you calm and present in the moment.

Enjoy the uplifting sounds and use the tools wherever you go. Almost one hour long, the CD has five tracks, including a complete guided meditation.

Living in the Present Moment: Everyday Tools & Practices CD is available at:

www.LivinginthePresentMoment.com

Made in the USA
Middletown, DE
20 October 2022